And So I th

Khathija Ismail

BookLeaf Publishing

And So I thought..... © 2022 Khathija Ismail

All rights reserved.

No part of this publication may be reproduced, stored in a retrieval system, or transmitted, in any form or by any means, electronic, mechanical, photocopying, recording or otherwise, without the prior written permission of the presenters.

Khathija Ismail asserts the moral right to be identified as author of this work.

Presentation by *BookLeaf Publishing*

Web: www.bookleafpub.com

E-mail: info@bookleafpub.com

ISBN: 9789357692304

First edition 2022

*I dedicate this book to all my loved ones
who are the reason for who I am today.
Thank you*

Seasons

Branches on the tree stretching majestically,
Blossoming with buds of joy,
Adding strokes of colours
For life to enjoy.
Beaming with radiance
And Covering the horizon with its fragrance.
The scent permeates the skin
Awakening every cell once dead.
Feeling full of energy
Rejuvenated
The girl skips back home merrily.
Unable to believe the magic.
Anticipating her next visit
She races back swiftly,
To once again embrace the spell boundlessly.
Rushes towards the tree
Only to find what once stood there
Majestically has completely crumbled and fallen tragically.
The season has changed
And everything is has been buried.

And so has my marriage!

Searching

Today once again,
I realise that I need to step out on this path alone.
I have to focus on my goal alone.
I have to walk alone.
With courage
Boldness
With determination.
And although I've done it many times before,
And although I've versed this path before,
I have to traverse alone.
My heart can't help it,
It goes looking for support,
Although, it knows there's no solution.
So once again today I tell myself:
You're traversing this path alone.

Redefined

I don't know what I am feeling towards you. Not anger nor happiness. Just numb.
My connection with you has been redefined.

I started my life with you,
Thinking our bonding was a perfect two.
You were an ideal match,
Too precise and an accurate attach.
Your love fathomed deeper, through the depth of my soul.
Your laughter,
Your love,
Your hugs and kisses,
All Your daily dosage, which never misses,
of course our pleas and cries, once in a while.
I cherished you into my palm, carefully, even before I carried my child.
There weren't any days that went by without me being grateful for such a blissful fairy life.
Somedays weren't shining , but that was fine,
I knew whatever happens you were there to say it's alright, ure mine.
Years went by and we settled in to our family life.

We shifted from a young married couple, to middle aged wine.
Four beautiful flowers bloomed our path,
Singing melodies and cheering us,
Bringing a new fragrance to our hearts.
A complete perfect family, just as I want.
Still, I took pride in how u shined.
And So I thought......
I thought
Life couldn't be any more fine.
All of a sudden, without any warning
life took it's stride,
Crashing me in with it's vicious tides.
Leaving me with no room, but to cry.
Everything was dropping down at a pace,
I had no choice but to race.
Not knowing why all this is happening in first place.
Only questions surging without any answers to replace.
Reason being, you weren't there to give me solace.
You were faraway from me.
Hiding In your own closets full of fears.
hallucinations and voices screaming in ur ears.
At that point in my life, I felt defeated.
Struck down and cheated.
Asking God the burning question....
Why me?

Why do I need to be tested?
Then quickly I realised that's Allah's decree,
I'm his servant who should submit to his creed.
still that doesn't answer any of my plea
What am I supposed to do with out any key?
Then finally you opened up and said the
PROBLEM WAS ME.
What do I do?
accept your answer?
If I do, then that would break me.
Thinking..... Wasn't my love for you true?
How could you be so ungrateful and turn everything blue.
Saying that I was ignorant and neglectful.
Anger fuming up and swallowing me in,
Failing to see the state you was in.
Silence was my weapon, as I coved into my shell.
Truly speaking, that was all I had as my spell.
I can't keep going like this for too long.
People questioning me for what was wrong.
I had no answer,
than to say my life was gone.
You tried Reaching to me
From inside your four white walls
It Became pointless when I dismissed all your calls.
You said I wasn't there
So I said I don't care

Who said I need to be fair?
Therapists tried to talk it thru
Reaching out for any clues
As to know why I became the problem for you,
Needless to say anymore
They reached out for their pen
wrote down bipolar stage 4.
Not having a clue what it was
All I knew was it was depression,
which had to have a cure.
I thought it was a phase
And u would get over it without a daze.
Few tablets could wash it away.
Surely, Its just little hiccup along our way.
Before I know it u would be OK.
You were discharged.
Something was missing when you stepped inside,
You were empty, distant with deep dark sorrows in ur eyes.
I was stubborn not to come and ask,
Because I knew I didn't want to face the task.
It wasn't a hiccup or a phase,
It was the harsh bomb I had to face.
The voices in your head returned again
With a greater impact and rage,
Trapping you further inside ur cage
Bouncing back and forth out of the hospital maze.

You were walking dead and a sleeping zombie
Basically an addictive druggie.
No income, but that don't mean the bills were all done.
one after the other,
holding on to survive thru this roller coaster.
I kept telling myself there's got to be light somewhere in this dark shelter.
kids smiles vanished
They were miserable and flustered
they tipped toed around us,
not to be noticed,
or else they might be gravitated into to this sharpnels.
six months past,
u sensed that u needed to break away,
promising me upon ur return tn u would not sway.
just as drained and anxious I let u ......
for the first time, I realised what was meant by time goes slowly for those who wait,
time was against me.
not a phone call or a text,
as I eagerly anticipated ur usual jovial msg.
Everytime I dialled the phone
I would hear myself shouting
as to why u are shutting me away
all u said was u were feeling numb,
a month past... Which seemed like a decade.

You finally returned just as promised
with a new facade.
kids jumping with joy,
I was with anger and hurt, all that melted down
with ur touch.
i knew at once it was my life and soul which
was bk
You ran faster and with fury on ur track,
you wanted to pick up life from wer u
wer trapped.
eliminating all the tablets
and getting back on to ur railway job .
there I hd it my perfect life bk once again.
no hospitals,
no therapies,
no episodes,
no tablets
everything finished,
so I thought.......
once again another missile struck
your workplace decided to give u a sack.
again fallen flat on our faces.
This time paralysed through out,
No words to succumb the surface of the sorrow.
You never showed any of ur hurt,
Nor did I, well to my ultimate best.
But deep inside we both knew it ripped us apart.
Struggles were just on going
I had barely any thing to cling

Patience to God's decree seemed just too thin.
I saw u bowing,
Prostrating to God with your head down.
So I thought....
Where did u manage to scrape
To find that atom weight of hope.
Oh well I guess it sparsely there,
For u to just about rope.
U landed a new job,
Things looked overall tidied,
But really just being deeply embedded,
U lifted yourself up,
Full of energy and spirit
Only to say 'I done this all by myself, I am an Atheist'
The reason for my chrisis Is u,
I had to rechannel my aggregation,
If not I would hate you.
Piled on top of many accusations
Which I was burdened already.
This is just another.....
So I thought....
This vicious cycle of tablets and depression wouldn't stop

Everything is Redefined.

Shards of Beauty

The beauty of being shattered is how the shards become our character.
This is how we are refined by our pain. When the storm rips you to pieces,
You get to decide how to put yourself back together again.
The storm gives us the gift of our defining choices.
You will be a different person after the storm.
The storm will heal you,
Far from your perfection.
People who stay perfect never really got to live fully .
You will not be the same after the storms of life;
You will be stronger,
wiser and more alive than ever before!!!!
Maybe our real life begins once we fail,
It humbles us,
Webecome a person of self conscious of our deeds.

Why do you keep going?

Why do I keep going?
I keep walking because behind every sun's setting is a rising.
Behind every storm is a Refuge.
Behind every fall is a rise.
Behind every tear is a cleansing of the eyes.
And in every spot you've ever been stabbed, is a healing,
and the creation of skin is it's stronger than it was.

Waves

I can't even count all the times I've been here:
Surrounded by waves with no idea how I'll be saved.
But it was always there.
Every Single Time.
No matter how dark it got.
No matter how massive the waves grew. No matter how impossible.
It was always there:
a light in the distance that made me keep going.
 That made me keep hoping. I learned every single time that Allah would never let me drown.
Never!
And that no storm lasts forever.
However strong I may demonstrate my faith in God, I too slip and start drowning in my waves,
 But I'm thankful to God for rising me up again.

Chambers

You can look at her but you'll find she is not
what you see.
She has hidden herself so much she has become
a women of mystery.
You'll have to unlock the Chambers of her heart,
But it wouldn't be easy.
She has given it back to her Creator,
Find Him and you shall find her.
Where she wishes to be.

Ocean's Blue

Are you swimming up stream in an ocean of blue?
Do you feel like your sinking?
Are you sick of the rain after all that you have been through?

When you can't take it, you can make it.
Sometime soon I know you will see,
Coz when you are in your darkest of hour
And when all the light just fades away

When your like a single flower whose colours have turned to shades of grey,
Hold and be strong
Taking each step at a time,
dont loose your spirit or sway.

Light

Drenched completely in gloom
For there is no you to take me through.
Digging deep inside for the light
Which I once knew.
I guess it flew
As the darkness grew.

Mind

Sometimes I forget
What matters and what doesn't
Who matters and who doesn't
My mind knows
But I'm trying
To teach my heart.

Pathways

Different pathways
Are never easy,
It's messy
It's difficult.
I'm glad we were able to part ways
On negetive terms
Then the positive.

Patchwork

A patchwork quilt,
my memories of you
stitched together
to make sense
of life without you.

Each square
lined with the pain and love,
Some days, I can't even look at it
without falling apart at the seams.

But some days,
I pull it down
and wrap it around me,
comforted that there's
still warmth to be found
in these often-painful memories.

Because the underlying thread
was love,
no matter how it seems.
The love will be what warms you
and holds you close through this bad dream.

Strength

Empty words
Empty feelings
Empty heart
Empty love
So my journey starts......
I found my purpose
I found my peace
I found my happiness
I found my strength
Did I loose anything....
Nothing at all
Have I gained?
Most Definitely yes
Gained the impeccable!
So navigate through
Guide and be grateful
For it is only Allah
You are answerable to!

Hope

Hope is never a mistake.

It is not foolish or naive.

To have hope is to be brave.

It is to see the darkness of the world,
and yet proclaim My Lord is Greater.

To believe fully and so deeply in God that you know He will give you.

And so the good and the bad blend into one much greater experience-
The experience of drawing near to Him regardless of what has happened to you.

Hope. Hope is never a mistake.

Darkness

As I close my eyes.
Try to think.
I feel Frozen and paralysed
Heavy and dawned inside.
At a standstill without any life.
Faint air without no sound
Ripping itself through the ground.

Time

Time is unstable.
And this terrifies us, or pretend
So we try to escape.
Or hang on...to anything.
To anything that we think can hold our world still.
Anything that can make time stop.
We are desperate to make time stop, so we don't have to lose...
Health,
Wealth,
Beauty love or life.
We are terrified of it slipping
away.
So we hide.
Pretend.
Numb.
Escape....And then cling. To anything.
Just to be saved from what terrifies us most:
Time and Change.
But God made it so everything would be unstable. Except Him.
A way to force us Home.
A way to push us to Shelter.

The only Shelter that doesn't shake or change or fade.

"By Time, indeed man is in a state of loss. Except those who believe and act righteously. And enjoin one another to Truth. And enjoin one another to patience." (Quran 103:1-3)

Mother

The strength of a mother is second to none ❤
Even when she is in time of stress,
when she is fighting her own demons, when she is beyond exhaustion
nothing will stop her from finding the strength she needs,
Just For her children to be at ease.

Tunes

My heart is a piano,
Raging with different tunes,
Difficult to capture a single note,
Tirelessly running,
Exhaustively playing
Falling down for mercy
To catch a moment of breath
Or even death.

Mostly it's just a bunch of spews
Tangled up in the most enraged hues.
Rushing,
Racing,
Rearing
Without any clues.
I wish I could play my music
With the crevice of energy,
Its not allowing me to.

I can't say no more
Im locked and sealed
Oceans of Tears dried up.
Drowning me deep to bury me alive

Kept the score

For so long,
I held back
I tested,
I kept score,
I counted,
I recounted,
I withdrew,
I shut down,
I retreated.
To what I considered my safe space:
nonchalance
disdain
contempt
dismissal.
It's so much easier not to care
If you tell yourself you don't care.
But you will never taste love that way.
Without the opening
The giving
The sharing
The trust
You will never know the blessing of the true
garment.
So
One day my soul just opened up

And all was lightness
And warmth
And kindness
And empathy
And concern
And grace
And the love flowed...

Phases

Moments will come and go.

Your pain will rise and fall.

Even your faith will see its' lows, But let the coming and the going,

the rising and falling,

the winning and losing

see you in beauty,

even as you are surrounded

by the seasons of life

and love

And even the winters of your heart.

Walls

She built walls

because she's been hurt deeply

and she is a guarded girl now.

Life and love have left her

suspicious and untrusting.

She's heard it all you know,

and worse than that,

she's seen it all.

She's been through more

than you'll ever know,

and she may share

bits and pieces of her story,

in the hopes that you might

understand her a little better,

But she won't share everything.

She will keep the rest buried beneath the fear of pain, humiliation, and judgment.

Milton Keynes UK
Ingram Content Group UK Ltd.
UKHW020756080124
435661UK00018B/1184

9 789357 692304